SARAH ST JOHN

Frugalpreneur

How to Launch, Manage, and Market Your Online Business for Under $100 Per Month

First published by Preneur Press 2019

Copyright © 2019 by Sarah St John

All rights reserved. No part of this publication may be reproduced, stored or transmitted in any form or by any means, electronic, mechanical, photocopying, recording, scanning, or otherwise without written permission from the publisher. It is illegal to copy this book, post it to a website, or distribute it by any other means without permission.

Sarah St John asserts the moral right to be identified as the author of this work.

Sarah St John has no responsibility for the persistence or accuracy of URLs for external or third-party Internet Websites referred to in this publication and does not guarantee that any content on such Websites is, or will remain, accurate or appropriate.

Designations used by companies to distinguish their products are often claimed as trademarks. All brand names and product names used in this book and on its cover are trade names, service marks, trademarks and registered trademarks of their respective owners. The publishers and the book are not associated with any product or vendor mentioned in this book. None of the companies referenced within the book have endorsed the book.

Affiliate Disclaimer: Certain products or services mentioned within this book may be affiliate links, which means I make a commission on any purchases made from those links. This is of no additional cost to you. I only recommend products and services I either currently use or have used in the past and feel is of value and relevance to my audience and readers of this book.

First edition

ISBN: 9781728665382

This book was professionally typeset on Reedsy.
Find out more at reedsy.com

Contents

Foreword — viii
Introduction — xi

I LAUNCH

Why Should I Have An Online Business? — 3
Write a Book — 8
Content Creation — 11
Affiliate Marketing — 14
Product Creation — 17
Drop Shipping — 19
Retail Arbitrage — 21
White a.k.a. Private Label Reselling — 22
Freelancing — 24
Offer a Service — 25
Direct Sales — 26

II MANAGE

Website, Landing Pages, and Sales Funnels — 31
Social Media Management and Scheduling — 38
Email and CRM — 40

III MARKET

Three Things to Convey in Your Marketing	45
Social Media Marketing	46
Text Message Marketing	49
Search Engine Optimization and Advertising	51
Other Forms of Marketing	53

IV WRAPPING UP

FAQs	61
Resource List	63
Acknowledgments	67
About the Author	69
Also by Sarah St John	71

To view the resources mentioned in this book in one place, please go to:
https://sarah-stjohn.com/resources

Check out some free courses at:
https://sarah-stjohn.com/courses

Check out the podcast that accompanies this book:
https://www.spreaker.com/show/frugalpreneur

Pre-order the next book in this series here:
https://books2read.com/b/authorpreneur

S⊚cial Sharx

- Social media management, scheduling & analytics
- Online reputation monitoring & review alerts
- Social shopping carts, contests & deals
- Unlimited social media accounts, posting & queues

Save $20 Now

Use Coupon Code SAVE20

Get $20 off now with coupon code SAVE20 at SocialSharx.com

- All-in-one website, sales funnel and landing page builder
- Bump Offers
- Upsells/Downsells
- Popups
- Membership Sites
- Online Store
- Starting at only $11/mo

Get Your Free Trial Today!
No Credit Card Required

Get your free trial today! No credit card required. SiteSeam.com

Foreword

by CHRISTA BANISTER

While I'm hard-pressed to remember my iTunes password most days (or let's be honest, pretty much any configuration of letters, numbers, and special symbols required these days for social media, e-commerce, you name it); I remember the first time I wanted to be my own boss like it was yesterday.

Twenty years ago, long before Mark Zuckerberg started Facebook, and Twitter was nothing more than a bird call, I was a newly minted college graduate with a degree in journalism, two jobs, and a side hustle as a freelance writer, concert promoter, and booking agent in my new hometown of Nashville.

Having a few jobs was normal for the creatively inclined in Nashville, and I was one of the few who didn't move to Music City to be famous. I wanted to write about musicians, but the magazine I wanted to work for wasn't hiring at the moment.

Those student loans kicked in right on schedule. But before long, week after week with little sleep — and even littler to show for it monetarily — caught up with me. And one ordinary Wednesday afternoon in March, two hours before I'd drive twenty miles to the little bookstore where I made minimum wage as the music buyer, I daydreamed what life would look like if I was copywriting, concert promoting, and booking concerts without those pesky outside-the-home gigs. Needless to say, a dream was born.

But how does someone go from regular worker bee to being her own boss and, you know paying the bills, saving a buck or two, and eating from time to time?

In my case, the stepping stone was finally landing the job at the aforementioned music magazine I'd moved to Nashville. Five and a half years of writing, editing, and making valuable connections set the groundwork for a thriving freelance career once I was ready for a new challenge. Not long after going freelance, another dream came true when I signed a book contract and released two novels. Little did I know, the grueling part of writing the novels was the easy part. Knowing how to promote my work — and getting the proverbial "most bang for my buck" — was elusive and involved a lot of trial and error. I sold a decent number of books, but it was the hard (and slow) way.

These were valuable, even necessary, experiences to learn from. But what if I'd had access to an innovative and trusted resource like the book you're about to read? Let's just say it would've been a game-changer that would've helped me avoid a bunch of rookie mistakes. I could've been working so much smarter (rather than harder) and making far more strategic use of my advance from the publisher.

With Frugalpreneur, you're being given a backstage pass to future business success in one accessible resource. In a competitive world where every dollar counts more than ever before, Sarah St. John provides innovative ideas and proven strategies to launching, managing, and marketing your online business for less than $100 per month.

For less than what many people spend in gas or eating out in any given month, you can be your own boss. More than that, you can be your own boss and succeed. No more juggling multiple jobs or fruitless side hustles you're just hoping and praying will take off. You will learn how to effectively and efficiently use social media, the power of passive income, and so much more that I won't spoil for you here. And you know what? As a bonus, you'll even have fun while you're learning because Sarah is such an engaging, passionate resource.

Take it from a girl who wished this book released a good two decades before it did. If you've ever wished you could be your own boss, reading Frugalpreneur is a valuable first step.

—Christa Banister, full-time freelance writer, author, blogger, and her own boss since 2005. For more information, please visit www.christa-banister.com.

Introduction

Hello, my name is Sarah, and I'm an entrepreneur. That sounds like the kind of introduction you'd expect to hear at an addiction recovery meeting, but entrepreneurship IS my addiction.

Let me tell you my story . . .

It all started in 2008. I had 6 different jobs that year. Things just weren't working out, so I started a business. And before you ask, the answer is yes—I continued to work a regular full-time job to pay the bills. I wouldn't suggest quitting your day job to pursue your business full time if you're just starting out. Wait until you're making enough from your side hustle or gig that it can replace your full-time income. Since then, I've started close to 20 different businesses while having ideas for at least another 20. I'll be honest. Some were and still are successful, and some bombed. Not so much because the ideas were bad (although there were a few of those), but because I didn't have the time, money, connections, or resources to launch some of those business ventures. But, that's okay. Sometimes you have to learn from your mistakes, regroup, and try something else. Even the most successful entrepreneurs and business owners will tell you that some of their ventures failed. It's rare for someone to get it right the first go-round.

I had a photography business for about 7 years, primarily photographing weddings. But while I enjoyed photographing animals, landscapes, and architecture, I eventually realized I didn't enjoy photographing people, which is the primary way of making money as a photographer, unless you get a gig for a magazine or something. In addition, I learned that photographing weddings was very time consuming. Sure, the wedding day itself only required actively taking photos for 4 to 8 hours, but the sheer time spent editing afterward drastically reduced my dollar per hour rate. Not to mention how expensive it is to maintain and upgrade camera equipment. It's not just the camera itself, but also the lenses, the memory cards, the lighting kits, the software, the classes. Also, I discovered that everyone and their dog was becoming a photographer. It seemed to be the new go-to method of self-employment. Not that there's anything wrong with that per se, but it diluted the market, and made for stiff competition. Needless to say, I wanted to do something else. Ideally something online, and something that cost less than $100 per month to operate.

But it's through these experiences I've learned that I've always been an entrepreneur at heart. It's in my blood. Perhaps you could say I was born this way. As a young kid, I'd take things I got for free (e.g., pencils, candy bars, etc.) and try to "flip" them by selling them to my friends so I could profit. Even today, I'm constantly looking for ways to flip things like sold-out concert tickets (Stub Hub is my friend). With each new business I launched, the entrepreneur in me became more prominent. I devoured every book on business or entrepreneurship I could get my hands on. I joined entrepreneurial Facebook groups and mailing lists, watched webinars, took online courses, and listened to podcasts. The more I learned, the more I yearned to learn. In all my failures as an entrepreneur, I never gave up, I'd just move on and try something else.

However, I got stuck. A turning point for me was during one of Dave Ramsey's "Financial Peace" classes. If you're unfamiliar with it, "Financial Peace University" is a 9-lesson course that teaches you how to pay off your debt and save via the snowball method. I wholeheartedly recommend the course. It's an eye-opening game changer. But as I sat there in class, I thought, "These strategies to pay off debt and save money are great, but what about also MAKING MORE MONEY to achieve your financial goals versus merely relying on your current income?" Then a light bulb went off in my head, and this is how the concept of Frugalpreneur began. I've spent the last few years testing out different ways to make extra money online while on a tight budget, so why not save other people a lot of time, money, and headaches, and teach what I've learned? I am the Frugalpreneur, and you can be one too!

So, what's your story? In other words, why do you want to become an entrepreneur?

Maybe you're looking for a way to make some extra cash on the side for spending money.

Maybe you're looking for a way to build up your savings, pay down your debt, or both.

Maybe you're wanting to create multiple passive, residual, and scalable income streams.

Maybe you're looking for a way to work from home so you can spend more time with your family and avoid rush hour traffic.

Maybe you're looking for more financial freedom.

Maybe you're looking for a way to get out of the nine-to-five office job rat race working to make someone else rich by instead working for yourself and earning an uncapped income.

Maybe you're a creative, business-minded entrepreneur who enjoys running your own company.

Or maybe you're like me and all of the above apply.

But, there's just one little problem—Money.

After all, you're interested in starting a new venture to MAKE money, not spend money. However, the saying "You have to spend money to make money" is true. At least to a certain extent.

In this book, I'll show you how to make money without going broke.

> *"It's completely possible to start on a very low budget without hindering the odds of success."*
>   – Chris Guillebeau

But, I want to take a moment to tell you what you can expect from this book.

My goal is to show you various ways to start and manage an online business on a tight budget. Many of the tools I'll discuss in detail are ones I use for my own businesses, and the majority are either free or inexpensive. I'll show you how, like me, you can reserve most of your business budget for marketing and advertising.

To summarize: I'll break down the different ways to make money online, detail and explain the must-haves for your online business, and share the best free or inexpensive tools and resources to help you succeed.

This book is short, but it's jam-packed with useful information because I don't want to waste your time. After all, the more time you spend reading this book, the less time you have to implement what I'm teaching.

So without further ado, let's get started.

I

LAUNCH

1

Why Should I Have An Online Business?

Imagine yourself on the beach in Aruba. You're sitting there, reading a good book, fruity concoction of choice in hand, waves peacefully lapping on the shore, palm trees swaying, and flamingos prancing past, when all of a sudden you hear your phone ding. You get mildly annoyed because you're on vacation, and everyone knows it because you've been blowing up your Instagram feed. Who in their ever-loving mind would dare to kill your vibe? You slide your sunglasses up your forehead as you squint at your phone—after all, the sun is BRIGHT in Aruba—and as the screen comes into focus, you start to smile. Your husband, or whoever you're with, tilts his sunglasses down and asks, why the smirk? You glance at him, pause for a brief moment, soak it all in, and say, "I just got my first sale." THAT, my friend, is passive income.

Reason Number One: Passive, Residual, and Scalable Income

> *"My favorite way to make money is while I sleep."*
> *– Tai Lopez*

Does the above quote sound too good to be true? It's not. There are many options to create something once that generates recurring passive and residual income, such as a book, or a course. Think about this: when you go to work for an hourly wage or a salary, you are paid for your time. Time is finite; therefore time is a commodity that is more valuable than money. It isn't possible to make more time, but you can always make more money.

Time is neither passive nor scalable. Scalable income is something you can create once, and it continues to earn you money over time without additional time being invested. If you work for an hourly wage or salary, there's only so much money you can make in a year or in your lifetime, and it always requires your physical presence. Wouldn't it be nice to be able to earn an uncapped income? Well, now you can.

So, with this in mind, a good way to decide if something is worth the cost associated with it is to ask yourself how long it would take you to manually do whatever this product or service does for you. Then multiply that amount of time by your hourly rate at your day job or even just how much you feel your time is worth. Is this product or service cheaper than that amount?

Or, an alternative question to ask yourself is: how much money could you make in that time frame working on something else on your list that earns money? Just because it's something you can do yourself, doesn't mean you should. Sometimes the sheer amount of time and effort something takes is longer than whatever you consider your going hourly rate to be worth. It's the same reason I pay someone to mow my yard even though I could do it on my own. Not that everyone should hire someone to mow their yard; that's not what I'm saying. But we all do something similar.

Think of going to a restaurant. Sure, you go there for the food because maybe you aren't the best cook in the world. But usually it's more about convenience. Sometimes you just don't want to spend time prepping, cooking, and cleaning up afterward, and feel it's worth the higher price to have someone else do all that work. Or maybe you hire someone to clean your house every two weeks. You could do it yourself, but you'd rather spend those two hours working on your business or something else. There are countless examples, but you get the gist. Everyone decides what it's worth to them to do something themselves or to hire outside help for.

Reason Number Two: Extra Money For Spending, Saving, or Paying Down Debt

Maybe you already have a full-time job, but you're only making ends meet or you want extra spending money, or both. Or maybe you want to make more money to build up savings or pay down debt. Sometimes the best or only way to save or pay down debt is to get an online side hustle.

Reason Number Three: Freedom and Flexibility

Maybe you aren't looking for supplemental income but instead you're looking for a way to make money online full time so you can quit your day job and stay home with your family, never needing to battle rush hour traffic again. Or maybe you'd like to travel the world or work unconventional, unsteady, or unpredictable hours that a normal job wouldn't tolerate. Maybe you only want to work 4 hours a week as Tim Ferriss suggests in his book by the same name. Or maybe you want to have a way to continue earning money after retirement.

I know several people working retail or office jobs into their nineties. There's certainly nothing wrong with this as long as you're working because you enjoy it. But if you aren't retired and continuing to work because you HAVE to in order to pay your bills, that's completely different. Don't misunderstand me here.

There's nothing wrong with working past retirement age if you're choosing to do so to keep you busy, or because you enjoy it, or because you don't know what else you'd do with your time. But let's say you're physically or mentally declining, or both, and really shouldn't be working, but you have to in order to pay the bills, not because you want to. What then? I want to create a future for you where this isn't a scenario. Sure, that means saving the extra money you do make now, but it can also mean finding ways to make passive or residual income as well.

So, to recap, 3 of the top reasons to make money online are: (1) to earn residual and passive income, (2) earn extra income, or (3) to gain work independence, freedom, and flexibility.

If you're like me, all of the above apply. But now you're probably wondering HOW you can make money online. There are a multitude of ways to make money online, but the ones I'll give you a brief overview of in this book are:

1. Writing Books
2. Content Creation (Blogs, Podcasts, Courses)
3. Affiliate Marketing
4. Product Creation
5. Drop Shipping
6. Retail Arbitrage
7. White a.k.a. Private Label Reselling
8. Freelancing
9. Offering a Service
10. Direct Sales

"If plan A fails, remember that you have 25 letters left."
  – Chris Guillebeau

In other words, I'd recommend trying out a few of these to see what your best fit is. I've tried several of these but have discovered I only enjoy about half of them.

2

Write a Book

"Don't watch the news . . . make the news. You don't read the newspaper, you write newspaper articles. You don't read books, yeah, you read books, but learn to write them." – Grant Cardone

One way to make money online you maybe haven't thought about or considered is by writing a book. Yes, writing a book. You may think it's out of the realm of possibility. But I believe we are all experts in something or have a story to tell, and others can benefit from our varied knowledge.

I had the idea for this book a couple years ago. It came to me out of nowhere. I heard myself say something like, "I've done so much research on how to run an online business on a budget, that I could write a book about it." Seconds later, I also said, "In fact, I think I will." So I did. Now, I know not everyone is that quick to jump on their book idea. Most people don't even realize they have a book in them, and even if they do, think they could never actually write it because they either have no idea how to, are too scared to do so, feel they don't have the time, or a million other reasons.

Is there something that you've repeatedly been told you're good at? Is there something you've researched extensively? Is there something you've studied or went to school for? Maybe you're a creative person who dabbles in writing fan fiction. Whatever it is, we all have something we're an expert in whether we realize it or not. So why not share that with the world and make an impact while simultaneously making money off it, or building a brand and business around it?

There are two basic reasons people read a book: entertainment (fiction), or education (nonfiction). If you're good at storytelling, I'd recommend writing fiction. If you're more facts and figures oriented, I'd recommend writing a nonfiction book whether it be about business, education, finance, self-help, etc.

Now, I know what you may be thinking: "Sarah, that sounds way too complicated, expensive, and time consuming. And who will publish my book?" You! That's right—you! We're in an interesting time now with the proliferation of self-publishing. There are a few companies who self-publish, but I use KDP Publishing by Amazon (formerly called CreateSpace). It's free to publish and you even get a free International Standard Book Number (ISBN) assigned. You don't have to order a bunch of books and store them. With no need to keep an inventory, there are no upfront expenses in that regard. Everything is printed on demand. Any time someone orders your book, Amazon prints it and ships it. It's that simple. Amazon = Amazing!

Note: I'd be remiss if I didn't mention that I have another book coming out later this year solely on the topic of self-publishing. If you're interested in learning more about the steps to successfully self-publish and launch a book, check out my next book in this Preneur series: *Authorpreneur: How to Self-Publish and Launch a Book to Build your Business.* I go into much more detail in that book than I do here.

Now, let's discuss the advantages and disadvantages of writing a book.

Advantages of writing a book: If you have a creative personality that likes to produce content, then writing a book would certainly fulfill that creative itch. It's also original. Sure, there may be other books out there on your topic, but no one is coming at it from your unique angle and telling it the way only you can. It's always good to have a lot of different perspectives on the same topic. Why do we have so many fast food burger joints, and more importantly, why do they all pop up on the same street corners as each other? There's room for many people in the same space, which is a good thing because it shows there's a market for it. So, don't let competition deter you. Another advantage is that a book is a good introduction to you and your business. It's a glorified business card, if you will, and also creates instant credibility and authority in your niche. I discuss this in more detail in the aforementioned book, *Authorpreneur: How to Self-Publish and Launch a Book to Build Your Business.*

Disadvantages of writing a book: The only disadvantage of writing a book is time. It's one of the most time-consuming things you could do. But guess what? It may be a lot of work up front, but can provide a royalty check every month for years to come. The best part? Your copyright exists 70 years beyond your death. This means your children and grandchildren could be earning monthly checks from your book(s). Talk about leaving a legacy!

Here is a helpful resource:

30 Day Book Boot Camp ($197 onetime fee) https://rebrand.ly/30dbc

3

Content Creation

Blogging and Podcasting

Maybe the idea of writing a book sounded appealing, but you don't want to write an entire book. Consider starting a blog or podcast, or making guest appearances on other people's blogs and podcasts, or both. Blogging and podcasting are similar to a book in that you're sharing your expertise, just in a different format. Some people prefer information in smaller doses (blogging) or via audio (podcasting) so that they can digest the content while they multitask with house chores or commuting to work.

You don't get paid up front by blogging and podcasting, but you can use affiliate marketing within either so long as it relates to what you're discussing. We'll cover affiliate marketing in a bit. Or if you have more of a service and solution type of business, you can get the word out via blogs and podcasts.

For blogging, you'll need a website, and I discuss websites later in this book.

For podcasting, you'll need a podcast hosting platform. I personally recommend either Podbean or Spreaker as they have the best rates and most user-friendly interfaces, in my opinion, but there are several platforms to choose from.

Here are some useful podcast training courses:
- Free Podcast Course (free) https://rebrand.ly/freepodcastcourse
- Podcast Success Academy (free) https://rebrand.ly/psa
- Podcasters' Paradise ($97 per month) https://rebrand.ly/pparadise
- Power Up Podcasting ($799) https://rebrand.ly/pupodcast

Course Creation

"I quickly learned that the key was to release more information products. My income would take a major jump every time I expanded my arsenal of online courses."
   – Anik Singal

A more profitable form of content creation is creating online courses, training, or both. Online courses and training usually consist of both audiovisual and written information. You can either appear in front of the camera and use something like a whiteboard for the visual part of your teaching. Or you can do a screen-share recording instead. In addition, it's advisable to include some downloadables and worksheets for your students for continued learning.

There are several places to create and host online courses and training. For instance, you could do it through an educational marketplace such as Udemy. The best thing about Udemy is that since it's a marketplace, anyone and everyone can find and take your courses.

But I prefer using a platform such as Thinkific, Teachable, or Podia. These aren't marketplaces, but the user experience and platforms are so much simpler and user friendly.

Of the three, I recommend Thinkific because you can create your first 3 courses for free, plus they don't charge transaction fees. Teachable's plans start at $29 per month, and unless you opt to pay for a higher tier of service, they charge 5% in transaction fees. Podia's plans start at $39 per month, and while Podia itself doesn't charge any transaction fees, expect to be charged a fee of 2.9% + 30¢ by the payment processor (either Stripe or PayPal). However, both Teachable and Podia are worth considering if you have more than 3 courses.

The advantages of content creation: Minimal original investment; the ability to create an audience plus grow a following.

The disadvantages of content creation: Time consuming, but also consider a possible learning curve with new technology if you'll be podcasting, creating courses, or both. If you are shy or introverted, overcoming your nerves might also present an issue.

Speaking of courses, below is a list of a few free courses I recommend. If you want to view them all in one place, you can just go to: https://sarah-stjohn.com/courses

- Affiliate Profits Club
- E-Marketers Club
- Membership Marketers Club
- Power Copy Club
- Power Marketers Club
- Product Profits Club
- Success Upgrade Club
- Web Profits Club
- Wealth Upgrade Club
- Traffic Generation Club

4

Affiliate Marketing

Affiliate marketing is where an online retailer pays a commission for traffic or sales generated from its referrals. This is one of my preferred methods of making money online.

Some online retailers, such as Amazon, host their own affiliate program. Companies who host their own affiliate program may refer to it in these terms: affiliate, partner, or referral program, but they all mean the same thing.

Then there are companies who use a third-party affiliate marketing program. With these companies, I recommend creating an account and searching by categories you're interested in referring and then signing up for each individually. This is the best way to get started if you aren't sure yet which specific companies you want to work with. Here is a list of several third-party affiliate marketing companies: Avangate, ClickBank, CJ Affiliate, Fast Spring, Has Offers, iDev Affiliate, Impact Radius, JVZoo, Paddle, Partner Stack, PayDotCom, Pay Kickstart, Rakuten Marketing, Refersion, Rewardful, ShareASale, Tap Affiliate, WarriorPlus, and Zaxaa.

There are two main ways to use affiliate marketing. The first is to refer relevant products to your audience or customers via content such as blog posts and podcasts. I'd recommend going this route if you already have a fan base, audience, customers, or a following on a particular topic or niche. It's simple to refer relevant products you know your customers may be interested in. This is the way I like to do affiliate marketing. The other method applies if you don't have a business customer base, following, or niche. With this route, you'd do affiliate marketing through various Google and Facebook ads.

Note: I don't like or recommend the second method because it's more expensive, since you must pay for ads to get traffic or clicks. I'm also not interested in spending my hard-earned money to promote someone else's products I most likely don't even use. Whereas with the first method I described, you don't have to pay for ads (though you certainly can if you want to reach a broader audience) and you have a more vested interest in the product or service because it's one you use (or have used in the past) and recommend. Additionally, I only enjoy affiliate marketing when I know I'm offering a valuable resource to the right audience. It gives it a purpose beyond just being a way to make passive money.

Now, let's discuss the advantages and disadvantages of affiliate marketing.

Advantages of affiliate marketing: You don't have to create, keep, or maintain an inventory of your own products or services. But unlike drop shipping (which we'll get into in a bit), affiliate marketing isn't just for physical products. It can be used with services, courses, coaching programs, software as a service (SaaS), etc.

Disadvantages of affiliate marketing: Other than the fact you aren't creating your own product or service (which can be a good thing), I see no significant disadvantages to affiliate marketing. It's one of my favorite ways to make passive money—and can be one of the most profitable.

Note: If you're wondering if a particular company has an affiliate program, it will likely be hyperlinked at the bottom of their website or listed on their "About Us" page. If you're unable to find any information there, contact support and ask if they have an affiliate or referral program.

Tip: When promoting an affiliate offer always include a disclaimer stating that you make a commission on sales through your affiliate link, but then also assure your audience that you only recommend products or services you or someone you know has used and finds useful and relevant.

Here is a list of some useful affiliate marketing training:

- Affilorama (free) https://rebrand.ly/aff
- Affiliate Profits Club (free) https://rebrand.ly/apc
- 123 Affiliate Marketing https://rebrand.ly/123am

5

Product Creation

Are you creative and good at making products such as jewelry, paintings, drawings, and the like? Then this would be an avenue you should consider.

Word of caution: don't expect to get rich doing this, at least not overnight. Creating and selling products is the most time-consuming and generally the least profitable way to make money online when you consider dollar per hour spent, but if you have something you're good at making, go for it!

This category is pretty self-explanatory, so let's jump right into the pros and cons.

The advantages of product creation: Ability to be creative without as much competition because your product is original.

The disadvantages of product creation: Time consuming; initial expenses for supplies; the lowest profit margin in terms of making money online.

Tip: There are several e-commerce options you could sell your products on, but I recommend an e-commerce solution with a built-in marketplace where people can search and find your products. Examples of this would be Etsy, Storenvy, or Tictail. For making or designing T-shirts, you could use Printful, Teespring, Spreadshirt, or Zazzle. I personally prefer and use Printful for creating, and Storenvy for selling.

6

Drop Shipping

Drop shipping eliminates the need of maintaining an inventory as you partner with a drop shipping wholesale supplier and list their merchandise for sale. The other nice thing about drop shipping is that you don't have to handle the shipping either.

For drop shipping, I recommend setting up a Shopify storefront ($29 per month for the basic plan) and then adding the apps Oberlo, Dropwow, and Ali Express. These apps will give you access to thousands of wholesale products you can drop-ship. But a word of caution: pick a niche. Don't just offer everything under the sun. You need to specialize so you can appeal to a certain market or demographic. If you try appealing to everyone, you won't reach anyone. I had a drop shipping business for a while focusing on baby and toddler clothing. The reason I chose this niche, other than being cute and fun, was because of low shipping costs (often allowing me the ability to cover the costs of shipping and offer free shipping to customers), and low return rates due to requesting or receiving the wrong size (improbable with infant and toddler clothing, unlike adult sizes that vary wildly), or due to breaking (unlike bigger, bulkier, or fragile items).

But, drop shipping wasn't for me because I wasn't creating something original or unique. I was just selling discounted stuff at a markup. Also, there's a lot of drop shippers out there, and it's hard to compete with Amazon or other online retailers. Ultimately, I knew I wanted to do something more creative, so I dropped drop shipping.

Advantages of drop shipping: No inventory needed; no shipping; no need to create your own products.

Disadvantages of drop shipping: Lots of retailer competition and not particularly fulfilling if you're the creative type.

Tip: When setting up an online storefront, be sure to take advantage of the various free or cheap third-party plugins that will help with cart abandonment. If you're using a Shopify store (or any other eCommerce platform), I recommend Beeketing or POWr.io.

7

Retail Arbitrage

Retail arbitrage sounds like something illegal, doesn't it? But the good thing is that it's not illegal. Retail arbitrage is when you buy clearance products either online or in a physical store, resell them online at the retail price, and then you pocket the difference. Popular sites include Amazon and eBay. I recommend Amazon for retail arbitrage because you can send the products to them, and they'll maintain your inventory for you. Whenever an item sells, you get paid. Also, if a customer has Amazon Prime, they can still take advantage of Amazon's Prime shipping.

Advantages of retail arbitrage: You don't have to create your own products. If you use Amazon, you don't need to ship directly to customers or maintain a physical inventory yourself.

Disadvantages of retail arbitrage: It requires a higher up-front investment in purchasing products. This is the main reason I haven't tried retail arbitrage. If I ever do, I'll be sure to tell you my experience via my blog.

8

White a.k.a. Private Label Reselling

White a.k.a. private label reselling is when you sell another company's service under your own brand as if you're the original creator. Companies that offer white label reselling are usually software as a service (SaaS). White label reselling requires either a monthly or annual fee, and those fees can vary from a few hundred dollars a year to a few hundred dollars a month. However, it's always cheaper and easier going this route than creating your own software and selling it. With white label reselling, companies are responsible for all the developing, and you can contact them for any customer service needs. All you have to do is market it.

White label reselling is similar to affiliate marketing because you're referring and advertising someone else's product or service. The difference is that you're acting as the owner of the company and must pay a licensing fee for the ability to resell their product or service, whereas there's rarely a fee to refer affiliate products and services. Also, with affiliate marketing, you're earning a commission percentage of sales, not the full amount, nor do you get to set your own pricing like you can with white label reselling.

The advantages of white label reselling: There is no cap or limit on income potential, and it could be quite lucrative.

The disadvantages of white label reselling: It requires more capital up front. In addition, you must market products through your own company which means the added expense of additional ads and generating your own traffic.

9

Freelancing

Perhaps there's something you're good at and can crank out in rapid succession. Maybe it's creating logos, voiceover work, writing short articles or blog posts, proofreading, etc. You can offer your services on websites such as Fiverr or Upwork. People can search, find, and hire you based on your services, or people can post a specific job or project, and you can bid on the project.

The advantages of freelancing: Freedom and flexibility to work when, where, and how you want.

The disadvantages of freelancing: It depends on what type of freelancing it is and where and how you find your customers, but if you're offering your services through one of the websites mentioned above, you may not make a lot of money per gig because those site visitors are usually looking for a good deal. However, if you're speedy and can crank out several gigs a day, then it could yield a nice income.

10

Offer a Service

Are you an expert on something you can use to provide a service or solution? Examples: social media management, working as a virtual assistant or bookkeeping, online marketing, etc. Your options are working on a freelance basis, or getting hired on a part- or full-time basis by one or more companies. You can offer your services on a freelancing website if your service category is offered, create your own website, or both.

The advantages of offering a service: It's creative and original; you get to be your own boss.

The disadvantages of offering a service: Much more time consuming than other options, and therefore is not passive.

11

Direct Sales

Direct selling refers to selling products only obtainable through a non-retail environment via a representative of the company.

I've never done direct sales as it's not something that interests me. You generally have to purchase a starter kit which can be costly and offers no guarantee you'll be able to sell those items. In addition, you'll most likely be trying to sell products to people you personally know. But competition can be stiff if other people are selling the same products in your social circle. Think of selling Girl Scout cookies. How many times did you hear from someone you know, "Oh, I'm sorry, my coworker's daughter already sold me 72 boxes of thin mints. I'm tapped out". In addition, direct sales are not always something that can be done solely online as you are sometimes required to host parties and events to sell the products or services. For the purposes of this book, we're predominantly looking at ways to make money online. However, I know many people who do direct selling (and I'm sure you do as well), so I wanted to be sure to include it.

Some well-known direct sales companies are Herbalife, Mary Kay, Pampered Chef, Plexus, Rodan + Fields, Scentsy, and Tupperware.

Note: Multilevel marketing (MLM), also known as "network marketing" has a direct sales component to it. The biggest difference between being in direct sales versus an MLM is that with multilevel marketing you can earn money by recruiting other salespeople. That's fine so long as that isn't the primary goal or mission. The primary way to make money with direct sales should always be the selling of the product or service, not in gaining new team members.

What you want to stay away from are pyramid schemes. These are MLMs with no exchange of a product or service, and you only get paid for recruiting "team members." Be cognizant of the differences between direct selling, MLMs, and pyramid schemes, and always do your research.

II

MANAGE

12

Website, Landing Pages, and Sales Funnels

"As you market and grow your business you need your own piece of internet real estate. If you are building a business and purely using social media for your online presence then you are on rented land." – Chris Ducker

Unless you're an affiliate marketer with a niche audience, where perhaps just social media and a free blog site would suffice, then you'll need a website. Some companies think just having a Facebook page is enough, and while that's better than nothing, I personally believe a website is a necessity. For one, it makes you look more professional. If a company doesn't have a web presence, I'll rule them out and go with the competition. Does that sound harsh? Perhaps. But a website is the basic starting point to learn about a company, and if a company doesn't have a website, then I'll move on to a company who does. Second, a website helps search engines find you easier. Third, it's easier for customers to find the information they're seeking when it's all contained in one centralized, organized location (e.g., pricing, directions, a menu). Fourth, the only way you can have a sales funnel is if you have a website or landing page (more on this in a bit).

While you can hire a web designer to build your website for you, it's unnecessary. There are plenty of simple drag-and-drop website builders on the market where you can create your own website in a matter of minutes or hours on some rainy afternoon. You can also hire someone to use a website builder for you if you have no interest in creating it yourself. This will still be cheaper than hiring a web designer to create your website from scratch.

But, welcome to 2019. With as easy and cheap as websites are these days, it's a simple decision, and there's no excuse why any business wouldn't have a website. As I mentioned, when people are weighing the competition, many people will rule out any companies that don't have a website because if they can't even nail down a website, what do potential customers have to go on to make decisions? It's just one more thing people look at when shopping around. Bottom line—If you don't have a website, and the competition does? Good luck.

Before you create a website, you will first need a domain name. I use 1&1 IONOS as my domain registrar because they include a matching domain name based email address of your choosing. **Note:** If your domain registrar or host doesn't offer a free custom domain name based email address, you can either create one through Gmail for Business for around $5/mo or get a free one through Zoho. Once you have selected your domain name, you can create and build your website.

There are two main ways to create a website. The first is to use an all-inclusive drag-and-drop builder (I'll discuss this more in a bit), or WordPress.org (NOT WordPress.com). **Note:** If choosing WordPress, you will also need a web host such as Blue Host or Site Ground. These are the two recommended by WordPress.

The main benefit of WordPress is its endless customization capabilities because the list of WordPress plugins is nearly endless. However, there are two main disadvantages of WordPress sites: there is a steep learning

WEBSITE, LANDING PAGES, AND SALES FUNNELS

curve (at least in relation to other options we'll discuss), and you have to get the majority of your plugins through third-party companies, and that can get expensive. For these reasons, I prefer using a site builder that has most of the plugins and widgets I need already in one place so I don't have to go to a third-party to purchase plugins.

The most popular drag-and-drop website builders are Weebly, Wix, and Squarespace. They also handle the hosting included in their plans. These drag-and-drop website builders are simple to understand, learn, and use. There isn't much of a learning curve, and all the apps and widgets you likely want or need are included or can be plugged in right from your dashboard. But, the downside is Weebly, Wix, and Squarespace don't offer sales funnels. This is where my company, SiteSeam, comes in to save the day. SiteSeam is a simple drag-and-drop website builder, specializing in sales funnels and landing pages. We also include e-commerce, blogging, and membership sites. And hosting and SSL is included.

With all this said...websites as we have come to know them, are dying. A regular website, which is what most of the drag-and-drop website builders can create, is just informational. But, if you want your website to WORK FOR YOU, it needs to have landing pages and sales funnels. This is yet another reason solely relying on social media like a Facebook page isn't sufficient if you want to sell or scale.

> *"You can't just place a few 'Buy' buttons on your website and expect your visitors to buy whatever you're telling them to purchase. That's just not how our brains work."*
> – Neil Patel

I attended a small business expo a while back, where one speaker discussed sales funnels. It was the first time I'd ever heard of those, and I recall thinking, "What the heck is a sales funnel?" When I thought of a funnel, I thought of the type of funnel used to put oil or other fluids in your car. A friend of mine thought of funnel cakes (Hi, Liz!). But no, I'm not talking about oil changes or pastries. I'll be honest, though, this kind of makes me want to go to the fair and get myself a funnel cake. Why don't we all pause for a funnel cake break? The book will still be here when you get back, so go right ahead!

Welcome back!

So maybe you, like myself back then, are wondering what a sales funnel even is. A sales funnel refers to the buying process that customers are led through when purchasing products or services online.

There are a few landing page and sales funnel builders out there, but they're designed more to incorporate into your current website, such as a WordPress site. In a WordPress scenario, the tools I'd recommend regarding landing pages and sales funnels are Leadpages (landing pages; pricing starts at $37 per month), ClickFunnels (funnels; pricing starts at $97 per month), or a much more affordable option is OptimizePress (landing pages; one-time fee of $97). I'd also recommend Profit Builder (starts at $47 one-time fee), or Thrive Themes ($19/month).

So here's the dilemma: you can have a website, or you can have a landing page, or you can have a sales funnel. But I have an all-inclusive solution. I have a company called SiteSeam, which offers ALL of those things in one place: website builder, landing page builder, and sales funnel builder. No longer do you have to use two or more services to get your desired result. I believe it's the most powerful drag-and-drop website, landing page, and sales funnel builder on the market, and that isn't just because I own it. It's what I use for all of my businesses, so I practice what I preach. Pricing is also significantly more affordable than the alternatives on the market. It's worth much more than I charge, but as the Frugalpreneur my goal is to help other entrepreneurs run their online businesses on a tight budget, so I've made it extremely affordable for that reason. Heck, I'll even throw in a 10% discount just for the readers of this book. You can use coupon code **FRUGALPRENEUR** at checkout.

Now that we've talked about the importance and necessity of having a website, let's look at the different website elements you should utilize in order to make your website work for you.

- **Landing Page**. Landing pages are used for lead generation. It's usually a single webpage or a simple, two-step funnel that someone is directed to after clicking a certain call-to-action (CTA) on an online ad. Landing page builder options: SiteSeam (friendly reminder that this is my company), Leadpages, or OptimizePress for your WordPress site.
- **Lead Magnets, Opt-ins, and Pop-ups** . . . oh my! A lead magnet or opt-in is something you offer for free in exchange for someone's email address so you can further market to them via email. Examples of a good lead magnet include a free e-book, infographic, course, training, webinar, worksheet, etc. Recommended lead magnet creator and generator: Attract.io or Beacon.by. There are several opt-in programs out there, but the two I use and recommend are Privy and Convertful. Both have free plans available. An exit pop-up is a message that displays to users as they're attempting to navigate away from your site. Typically this will offer a coupon, or a free downloadable in exchange for the visitor's email address.
- **Sales Funnel.** As mentioned earlier, traditional websites do little other than provide information. To convert sales and create customers, you need a website with sales funnel capability. There are a few funnels builders on the market, but most are out of the price range or budget that most of my readers are seeking. That's why I've created an affordable alternative, SiteSeam. Plans start

at just $11 per month. And as a reader of this book, I'm offering a special discount code for 10% off. In the discount code box, just use this code: **FRUGALPRENEUR**.

- **Contact Form**. A contact form allows people to reach you directly from the website versus having to email or call you. At the bare minimum, it usually has at least the following fields: name, email, and comment. It can also have additional fields for address or phone number, if applicable. Any website builder will have a contact form widget, but you can also create a customized contact form and embed it via HTML code. I use and recommend JotForm for this. They have a free plan available.
- **Chat and Chat Bots**. An online chat allows website visitors to communicate with you in real time without having to wait for a response via an email, support ticket, or contact form submission. I use Tawk.to for this because it's free. If you have the budget and the need for it Intercom is a good option as it has a chat bot feature. Note: A chat bot is what it sounds like: a chat robot. You set it up to answer frequently asked questions or send out promotions, and it then becomes a hands-free simulated customer conversation. Using a chat bot on your website or Facebook business page is becoming one of the highest converting method of promotion. For this, I recommend Mobile Monkey.
- **Social Proof**. Social proof is copying what other people do. If you're selling anything on your website, you should use a social proof tool, such as Prove Source. This helps new site visitors see that other people are purchasing your products or services and gives credence to what you're selling. We witness social proof in our lives nearly every day. Say you aren't sure which way to turn after leaving a parking lot, so you follow the other cars because you assume they know what they're doing or which way to go? That's social proof. Recently I witnessed this firsthand when I was leaving a friend's house. I turned one way and another car of friends followed because they assumed I knew where I was going. After all, we were in the

same community where I also lived. But we all ended up in a cul-de-sac. Man, I felt dumb. But that was social proof in action.

13

Social Media Management and Scheduling

> *"Any entrepreneur who achieves sustained success has systems and automation's (sic) in place to ensure stuff gets done."*
> – John Lee Dumas

Social media is the second must-have for an online business.

Facebook is the biggest and primary social media tool you must use. No other website on the planet has as many users as Facebook. In addition, Facebook is one of the best marketing avenues for entrepreneurs on a budget, which I'll address in more detail later.

Twitter is just like the status portion of Facebook. Any post you make can only be up to 280 characters. It's harder to get followers on Twitter, and there isn't as much interaction. Most companies use it for customer service-related issues.

LinkedIn is basically the "Facebook" for companies, businesses, and entrepreneurs. Unlike Facebook, which appeals to a wide variety of people and topics, LinkedIn is for professionals, business posts, and information. This is a good social media site for networking.

Pinterest is only essential if you're doing eCommerce (i.e., selling a product via drop shipping, Etsy, etc.), or blogging and writing articles you can pin. You can even post your products on Pinterest and people can buy from there.

Instagram is important if your business has a lot to do with photography. If you're a photographer, Instagram should be your second most-used social network behind Facebook. Or, if you're a travel agent such as myself, Instagram is great for showing off photos of the places you've visited. Instagram also works well for anything where photos are required to inspire a transaction, such as apparel.

There are other social media platforms, but these are the biggest ones.

Now that we've discussed the main social media platforms, how do you plan to manage all of them? Sure, you can do it all individually and daily, but that gets time consuming and exhausting. My recommendation is to use a social media management tool so you can schedule all your posts days, weeks, or months out at a time, and you can schedule them to post to all your social networks at once. You can set aside one whole afternoon per month doing this versus several minutes every day. When you get into a rhythm, it takes less time than doing it piecemeal. Also, this way you won't forget to do it or make excuses.

For this, I recommend my company, Social Sharx, which is one of the most affordable and robust social media tools on the market. Social Sharx offers so much more than just social media management and scheduling. We also offer reputation monitoring, review alerts, and social shopping. Social Sharx is available for $197 per year. But as a reader of this book, I'm offering a special discount for $20 off with coupon code: **FRUGALPRENEUR**.

14

Email and CRM

"The strength of your business is directly tied to the quality of your email list . . . "
– Amy Porterfield

Email marketing is a necessity and should be the next thing on your list after you have your website set up with lead magnets, sales funnels, and contact forms because you'll want to market to those new email leads. Like social media, you can also schedule email campaigns in advance. You can set up groups, sequences, and lists such as new subscribers. There are only two email marketing platforms that offer a free plan, and those are MailChimp and MailerLite. I'd recommend starting with one of these. The nice thing about MailChimp is they are the most well-known email marketing platform so they integrate with nearly everything. However, I've found it lacking for what I needed or wanted. I personally use MailerLite, which is one of the best options for writers due to its integration options. It also ends up being cheaper than MailChimp once you reach over 1,000 subscribers and have to start paying for the service. But, once you have a decently sized email list and need more features, then I'd recommend switching over to ConvertKit (pricing starts at $29 per month) if you're a blogger or content creator. If you're in eCommerce, drop shipping, or affiliate marketing, then

I'd recommend GetResponse instead. It's one of the most extensive email marketing platforms out there, and their pricing is competitive, starting at just $15 per month. They also integrate seamlessly with most things too.

Tip: I recommend using the double opt-in setting so you're sure that the people who sign up for your list want to be there versus someone else signing up for them without their permission or consent.

Next, we get to the Client Relationship Manager (CRM).

> *"The most valuable asset you can own is a well-maintained customer database, because people who've already bought from you are way easier to sell to than strangers."*
> *– Perry Marshall*

Once you get leads or customers, you'll need a place to keep track of their pertinent information. It's up to you how much information to gather on your customers, but whatever you decide, be sure to set up a customer profile for them in your CRM along with all the info you have on them. For me, my CRM looks like this: name, email, phone number, address, birthdate (to send out Happy Birthday emails), anniversary date (to send out Happy Anniversary emails), age, interests, special notes, etc.

I recommend either HubSpot or Zoho CRM, which both offer a plethora of other affordable and useful business management tools, some of which are free.

III

MARKET

15

Three Things to Convey in Your Marketing

Scarcity – You want to make sure your offer is scarce such as a onetime offer, or only available for a limited time or in limited supply. This makes people realize that they may only get this offer, product, or price right here and now because it's only available this way or because it will sell out.

Urgency – Scarcity helps with urgency because it shows that something is limited in supply or time, but sometimes you need to be specific and say something is only available for a limited amount of time or for a certain price for only so long. This creates a sense of urgency.

Exclusivity – Exclusivity isn't as important as scarcity or urgency, but it can be the icing on the cake. It implies that not only is something in short supply (scarcity), or available only for a limited time or a discounted price (urgency), but that it's only available to a certain customer because that customer is "exclusive, special, or a VIP."

Note: Don't apply any of these as a sales tactics if you aren't actually going to go through with it. You don't want to lie or cry wolf. Not only is it not ethical, but it devalues you and your business, and people will stop taking you seriously or at your word.

16

Social Media Marketing

Facebook and Instagram ads

One of the most affordable and effective methods of advertising and marketing in this day and age is through social media, Facebook in particular, and Instagram by extension. First, it's very affordable. You can advertise for as little as $1 a day, though I'd recommend starting at $5 a day because in my experience, $1 doesn't give you enough data to figure out what needs to change in your ad to make it more effective. But more helpful than the affordable pricing is the fact you can pinpoint the demographic to a T. You can narrow down who your ad will appear to based on broad demographics such as age, gender, and location, but you can get much more specific than that and market to people who like certain public figures and pages. You can even market to people who have had particular online activity and purchasing habits, or what they've recently done such as gotten married, had a baby, or taken a vacation. The niche-down possibilities are limitless.

Tip: When advertising via Facebook, don't forget to install your Facebook pixel code on your website. This is used to track people who click on your Facebook ads and are redirected to your website, and it helps with retargeting ads.

Facebook Messenger

In addition, I recommend using Facebook Messenger for marketing. This has a much better open rate than email marketing. Facebook Messenger has an average of an 80% open rate and an 20% click-through rate (CTR) vs about a 20% open rate and 2% CTR with email marketing. Why is it that Facebook Messenger yields such a high open, click-through, and conversion rate? Why is it so much higher than email marketing? Well, it's simple. People can get hundreds of emails a day, some of which go straight to their spam folder and will never even be seen. Even if your email makes it to their inbox, there are so many other emails competing for your customer's attention that your email will likely either go ignored, unopened, or worst of all: deleted without ever being opened. In contrast, people don't get nearly the deluge of Facebook messages. Also, that unread Facebook Messenger alert tends to bother people to see, and they'll want to clear those alerts by clicking on your message.

Now, don't misunderstand. You still need to be doing email marketing. Not all your customers will be on Facebook or use Facebook Messenger. It's also much easier to get someone's email address than access to their Facebook profile because they first have to message your page before your business page can send them anything via Messenger. Not to mention you can own email addresses, but you can't own Facebook data if they change their rules as they do from time-to-time. This is also why it's advised to have your own website instead of just depending on Facebook. Who knows if Facebook will be around in another decade? So, you need to keep email marketing, but so long as you can also market via Facebook Messenger, use it. It's a much, much smaller net to cast than email marketing, yet you will still receive better results per person on average via Facebook Messenger.

You can also create an automated funnel or bot within Facebook

Messenger. I recommend Mobile Monkey, but Many Chat is another good one. Best of all, both have free plans available.

17

Text Message Marketing

You thought the open rate for Facebook Messenger was good? Check out the open rate for text message marketing: 99%. You can't beat that. (Well, technically you can, but there's no such thing as a 100% open rate). People rarely receive text messages all day every day, like they do emails. Nor does it require them to be logged in to an app to receive the messages like Facebook Messenger. It pops right up to their phone, and they have no choice but to at least skim the message before deleting it, if nothing else. Text message marketing is a fraction of a penny per text, which makes it the most affordable method of marketing as well.

You can create automized text messages just like with Facebook Messenger or email marketing. I recommend Click Send (pricing varies with the amount of texts, but they will beat any cheaper quotes from competitors) for text message marketing.

IMPORTANT: Don't just start text messaging your customers. They need to opt-in to this marketing first. In addition, every text you send needs to have a way to opt-out within it, using the word "stop."

Social media and email marketing are still important, but the precipice of virtual marketing is now via text message and Facebook Messenger. Those yield higher open rates. Use them while you still can, because you never know when privacy rules will change.

18

Search Engine Optimization and Advertising

Google and Bing ads are also affordable, but the main way you pinpoint who your ad gets targeted to is all by keywords or search words. If what you're selling is either too broad or too specific, it won't work. It needs to be in the middle. If it's too broad, it'll be very expensive to appear in one of the first several search pages, and most people only look on the first page or two of search results. So too broad isn't good. But so specific that no one is searching for it is obviously not good either.

Let me give you some examples.

Too broad: *Web design.* Let's be realistic. If you're reading this book, you're on a tight budget, and you can't afford what it will cost to show up anywhere near the top of a search engine for something so broad that everyone and their mom, dog, and pet ferret are searching for.

Too specific: *T-shirts for dog trainers.* Something as specific as that would do much better being advertised on Facebook with niched-down audience demographics set up for dog lovers, dog trainers, etc.

Just right: *Wedding photographer in Dallas, TX.* Now, this may still be tough to get a top page result for, but it's at least doable because it's something people WILL search for. But, it's not too broad since it's a specific location. You'll need to be sure you include the city name and surrounding areas in your keywords and your ad title.

19

Other Forms of Marketing

Logo

Having a business logo is pertinent. You can create your own in Canva (free option available), but I'd suggest only using Canva for social media graphics and things of that limited nature, not logos, book covers, or anything that will be seen over and over again. Unless you're a graphic designer, I'd recommend hiring someone on Fiverr. Fiverr is a great resource for getting designs created by freelancers. Rates start at just $5, and there are a ton of professional designers.

Bookmark or Book as a Business Card

A business card is a must-have because it's tangible, cheap, and easy to hand out. Also, consider using a bookmark as your business card. A bookmark is only slightly more expensive and will not get thrown away as often as a regular business card. A bookmark sticks out and is useful, and if someone uses it in a book they're reading, they'll be reminded of your business. Bookmarks are particularly good if your business focuses a lot on photography (e.g. a photographer or travel agent). I use bookmarks as business cards for my travel agency.

But, do you want to take it to a whole other level? If you write a book, I recommend using those as your "business cards" instead. A book as a business card is much more impressive, and it guarantees someone won't just toss it or forget about you. Most business cards end up in the trash, but a book won't. Even if the person never reads your book, they'll see it lying around, as will anyone else who comes to their house or office, or they'll give it away to someone who may be even more of your target customer than they were. Heck, maybe they'll even sell it to a bookstore or at a garage sale. Who cares? As long as it's in someone's hands, or on display somehow or some way, that's all that matters. Sure, this costs more than a business card, but regular business cards tend to get thrown away. To print a self-published book costs about $4 on average, give or take depending on the number of pages. At some point, I plan to use this book as my business card for my other businesses outside of my travel agency.

Or aim for the best of both worlds: Use a book AND a bookmark to really impress.

Car Decal

Getting a car decal printed doesn't cost much. You could get one for as low as $20 through Vistaprint, or get one professionally made and affixed at a local print shop for starting around $150. But, think of how many people you would reach every day if you have a long commute or travel by car a lot. This is a super cheap way to advertise. You won't always be reaching your target audience, but maybe someone who sees it takes a photo or memorizes the info and passes it along to a friend. Regardless, you're bound to reach plenty of people every day, and that alone makes it worth the initial investment. Also, you pass a lot of the same people on your commute to work each day, and this daily reminder just ingrains your product or service in their mind. If they're your target audience, they'll eventually check out your website if they keep seeing it since it can take up to seven impressions before someone takes action. In contrast, online advertising and marketing will just reach someone once, or maybe a handful of times. But with a car decal, you could reach people 5 days a week, every week, for months or years. Think about what that constant reminder does. The onetime up-front cost for as many people as it will reach if you drive a lot will make your advertising impressions cost mere pennies or fractions of pennies after enough time passes.

Reviews and Testimonials

No matter what type of business you have, reviews are always necessary. The best way to get reviews is to find websites or bloggers in your niche who have done reviews in the past and contact them via email.

Tips: Aim to contact them via email instead of an online form as email is more guaranteed to reach them. Offer them your product or service for free and ask for a review within a certain time frame. Also, make sure to give them a deadline, or chances are they won't get the review done. They'll forget or move on to other things. Always ask that they email you their review, whether good or bad so you can know, grow, and learn from it. If it's good, ask if you can use it on your press page, or "as seen on" page (if it's a well-known site or blog). There are also review sites or directories you can use. It depends on what type of business you are in as to what type of review site or directory makes sense. When you have customers who have had a positive experience, ask for a testimonial that you can use on your website. Or people can submit reviews and testimonials directly on your Facebook business page.

Side note: While we're on this topic, if you are enjoying and learning from this book, do you mind reviewing it on Amazon or whatever site it was purchased on? I would greatly appreciate it! Thank you in advance.

Giveaways

Another good way to market your business, win over cold traffic, and gain new followers is to offer a free giveaway. I use KingSumo (free option available) for this, which makes it possible for contestants to share the contest via social media and email and get more entries that way. This is called a "viral giveaway."

Tip: Don't give away something that's highly desirable, yet generic (e.g., an Amazon gift card). Then anyone and everyone will be entering the contest. At first, you may think this is good because you'll get a lot more subscribers this way, but the problem is they aren't your target audience. You want to do a giveaway only your ideal customer or target audience would be interested in, so that the only people who sign up are potential future customers. You don't want your email list full of people who aren't genuinely interested in you or your business, because all they care about is a free Amazon gift card. The size of your email list isn't nearly as important as the quality of your email list.

Press Release

> *"The most effective way to build a brand is not by spending millions in advertising, but by finding a clever way to keep your name in the press." – Barbara Corcoran*

Another good way to promote your business, and for free or on the cheap, is a simple press release. You can use Web Wire (starting at $35 onetime fee) to distribute your press release to media sources. The nice thing about press releases is that if a big, well-known news source decides to run your press release, you can use their logo on your website, which ultimately adds to your credibility and image.

Tip: When applicable, make sure to add a media/press page, or an "as seen in/as featured in" page, or both to your website.

Network

Networking with other business owners may seem like an odd way to market, but if your business is in the business of helping other businesses (how many times can I say business in one sentence?), then this is important. You can join your local chamber of commerce, Facebook and Meetup groups, attend local business expos, etc. Many networking options are out there, most of which are free, so I'd recommend taking advantage of them. Even if you aren't in the business-to-business (B2B) space, networking is still important. You can usually find some sort of group or network within your niche. Even if you aren't meeting potential customers, it's good to get to know other business owners because you never know which business connections you may make and what sort of joint venture opportunities may come up as a result.

Guest Blog or Podcast

While having your own blog or podcast (or both) is great, you can reach more people by guest blogging or appearing as a guest on someone else's podcast. It's far easier and quicker to reach someone else's audience than to establish your own audience of a similar size, regardless of the number. But, don't just blog and podcast for anyone and everyone. Make sure the person already has an audience established, even if it's just a few people, and make sure that their blog or podcast is in your target audience or niche. You don't want to waste anyone's time, including your own.

Joint Venture or Collaboration

Along similar lines of appearing as a guest on someone else's blog or podcast, is to form a joint venture or collaboration with another entrepreneur who has a similar audience. Leverage each other's audiences by being on each other's podcasts, blogs, emails, etc. Or you can host a webinar, course, or summit together.

IV

WRAPPING UP

20

FAQs

Do I need to incorporate my online business?

I am not a lawyer, so I can't give you any legal advice. I'd advise you to contact a business attorney. However, I can tell you what I've done. I have several businesses, so what I've done is create one limited liability company (LLC) as my umbrella company and then have all my other businesses listed as DBAs (DBA stands for "doing business as") under that LLC. There are a few different legal structures to choose from, so it's best to consult a business attorney who can help break down your options or determine if you even need to incorporate. I incorporate as an LLC to limit my liability to just business assets instead of personal assets. I'd suggest that anyone doing business under any name other than your given name get a DBA at the minimum so you can open a separate bank account to keep business and personal funds separate. You can incorporate on Legal Zoom, or Incorporate.com (pricing for both sites varies accordingly).

What if I need to meet customers in person? Should they come to my house?

I know one of the primary reasons for having an online business is so you can work from home. However, depending on what type of business you're in, you may need to meet clients in person. If this is the case, you can always meet them at a Starbucks or some other local coffee shop. But if you need a physical office location for receiving mail, or access to conference rooms, podcasting rooms, meeting rooms, copiers, etc, then I'd suggest a coworking space such as Regus or We Work. You can also do an online search for local coworking spaces in your area. But Regus and We Work are the two main global ones with offices all over the world so you can even use their spaces as you travel. Coworking space starts around $50 per month and goes up from there, sometimes as much as $400 or more a month for a dedicated desk versus open seating, or up to $800 or more for a private office. If you don't need space often but would prefer a coworking situation versus a coffee shop, you can generally get a day pass for around $25/day.

Are there any legal disclaimers I need to include on my website or email marketing?

I would suggest including the following on your website footer: terms of use (or terms and conditions), privacy policy (include cookie policy and GDPR), and affiliate disclaimer (if you're doing affiliate marketing). Also, if you make any income claims, you need an income disclaimer. You can find templates for all of these disclaimers at Rocket Lawyer (pricing varies accordingly) and customize them to meet your needs. There is no need to include these in marketing emails, but always have a way for people to unsubscribe from your email list.

21

Resource List

To view the resources mentioned in this book in one place, please go to:
https://sarah-stjohn.com/resources

Check out some free courses at:
https://sarah-stjohn.com/courses

Check out the podcast that accompanies this book:
https://www.spreaker.com/show/frugalpreneur

Pre-order the next book in this series here:
https://books2read.com/b/authorpreneur

- All-in-one Website, Landing Page, and Sales Funnel Builder – SiteSeam (starting at $11 per month; 10% discount with coupon code **FRUGALPRENEUR**)
- Social Media Management – Social Sharx ($197 per year); $20 off with coupon code **FRUGALPRENEUR**)
- Affiliate Networks – Avangate, ClickBank, CJ Affiliate, Fast Spring, Has Offers, iDev Affiliate, Impact Radius, JVZoo, Paddle, Partner Stack, PayDotCom, Pay Kickstart, Rakuten Marketing, Refersion, Rewardful, ShareASale, Tap Affiliate, WarriorPlus, and Zaxaa.
- App Integration and Automation – Zapier (free plan available)

- Appointment Scheduling – Appointlet (free plan available)
- Courses – Podia (pricing starts at $39 per month); Teachable (pricing starts at $39 per month); Thinkific (free plan available); Udemy (free)
- Coworking Space – We Work, Regus (pricing varies accordingly; day passes start at $25; monthly plans start at $50)
- CRM, Customer Support, Ticketing – HubSpot, Zoho CRM, Zendesk (all have free plans available)
- Designer – Canva (free)
- Document Storage – Dropbox (free plan available)
- Drop Shipping Apps – Oberlo, Dropwow, Ali Express (all are free)
- E-Commerce Platforms – I recommend Shopify (pricing starts at $29 per month), but there are several out there
- Editing Tools – Grammarly, Pro Writing Aid (both have free plans available)
- Email Marketing – I recommend MailerLite for authors (free plan available), ConvertKit for bloggers or content creators (pricing starts at $29 per month) and GetResponse for e-commerce/drop shipping (pricing starts at $15 per month)
- Facebook Messenger – Mobile Monkey, Many Chat (free plans available for both
- Freelance Services – Fiverr, Upwork (pricing varies accordingly)
- Landing Page Builder – Leadpages (starting at $37 per month)
- Lead Generation and Reduce Cart Abandonment – I use and recommend Privy and Convertful (both have free plans available)
- Lead Magnet Generator – Beacon.by, Attract.io (both are free)
- Note-taking – Evernote (free plan available)
- Online Chat Box – Tawk.to (free)
- Online Marketplace Platforms – Etsy, Storenvy, Tictail, Zazzle, Amazon, eBay
- Payment Gateway – I use and recommend Stripe or PayPal (both have transaction fees but are free to use otherwise)
- Podcasting Tools – Audacity (free); Podbean (free plan available)

RESOURCE LIST

- or Spreaker (free plan available)
- Printed Materials – U Printing, Vistaprint (pricing varies accordingly)
- Quiz Makers – Interact (free plan available)
- Sales Funnel Builder – Click Funnels ($97 per month)
- Shopify Apps – Beeketing, Powr.io (free apps available)
- Social Proof – Prove Source (free plan available)
- Stickers and Packaging – Sticker Mule (pricing varies accordingly)
- Surveys and Forms – JotForm (free plan available)
- Text Message Marketing - ClickSend
- T-shirt Maker – Printful (pricing varies accordingly)
- Video and Web Conferencing – Zoom (free plan available)
- Viral Giveaways – KingSumo (free)
- Webinars – Demio, Webinar Ninja (pricing for both starts at $49 per month)
- WordPress Hosting – Bluehost, SiteGround (both pricing start at $4 per month)
- WordPress Plugins – Learn Dash (starts at $159 per year), OptimizePress (starts at $97 one-time fee), Profit Builder (starts at $47 one-time fee), Thrive Themes ($19 per month), Woo Commerce (free plan available)

Conclusion

I hope you found this useful, and that the information in this book will help you determine not only which online businesses to try, but also how to manage and market them. If you have any questions for me, please feel free to email me. I'll be launching a podcast shortly after this book is released and will attempt to answer questions via my podcast. Also, if you've found any of this information useful and implement it and have success with it, please email me to let me know. I'd like to use some case studies for podcast episodes. You can submit those to me at sarah@sarah-stjohn.com with the subject line "Case Study."

Review Request

Well, you've reached the end of the book, so I hope that means you've enjoyed it and learned something, even if it's just one takeaway you can implement today to grow your business. This is where I ask for a simple request. Would you be so kind as to submit an Amazon review (or wherever you purchased the book)? I'd love to hear your feedback, and every review helps.

Acknowledgments

God; my husband, Josh; my family: Mom, Dad, Tami, Tony, Lori, Jett, Creed, Sage, and extended family; my friends; my fans and followers; Christa and Kay – for all your help and advice in the writing process.

I'd also like to thank and acknowledge the following list of entrepreneurs for teaching me something:

Alexa Bigwarfe, Amy Porterfield, Anik Singal, Barbara Corcoran, Brendon Burchard, Brian Meeks, Brian Tracy, Bryan Cohen, Bryan Harris, Caitlyn Pyle, Carrie Green, Chandler Bolt, Charles Duhigg, Chet Holmes, Chris Ducker, Chris Fox, Chris Guillebeau, Chris Hogan, Christy Wright, Claire Diaz-Ortiz, Crystal Paine, Dana Malstaff, Danny Iny, Darren Rowse, Dave Chesson, Dave Ramsey, David Gaughran, David Siteman Garland, Daymond John, Derek Doepker, Derek Murphy, Donald Miller, Dorie Clark, Eric Ries, Frank Kern, Gary Keller, Gary Vaynerchuk, Grant Baldwin, Grant Cardone, Hal Elrod, Jaime Tardy, Jason Fried, Jay Papasan, Jeff Goins, Jeff Walker, Jim Kukral, Joanna Penn, Joel Friedlander, John Lee Dumas, Jon Acuff, Jonny Andrews, Joseph Michael, Julie Ball, Kelsey Humphreys, Kevin Harrington, Kevin O'Leary, Lewis Howes, Lisa Nichols, Lise Cartwright, Lori Greiner, Mark Coker, Mark Cuban, Mark Dawson, Matt McWilliams, Michael Gerber, Michael Hyatt, Michael Masterson, Michael Port, Mitch Matthews, Neil Patel, Nely Galán, Nick Loper, Nick Stephenson, Orna Ross, Pat Flynn, Paul Mahony, Perry Marshall, Peter Pru, Peter Voogd, Rachel Hollis, Ray Brehm, Ray Edwards, Richard Branson, Rob Eagar, Rob Kosberg, Robert Herjavec, Robert Kiyosaki, Robyn Crane, Russell Brunson, Ruth

Soukup, Ryan Deiss, Ryan Levesque, Sophia Amoruso, Steve Larsen, Stu McLaren, Tai Lopez, T. Harv Eker, Tim Ferriss, Tim Grahl, Tony Robbins, Trevor Crane, Trey Lewellen, Wesley Atkins, Verne Harnish, and Zig Ziglar.

About the Author

Sarah St John is an entrepreneur, writer, animal lover, and world traveler. Sarah has created several startups throughout her entrepreneurial career, and she currently owns a travel agency (palmtreetravel.net), a web design company (siteseam.com), and a social media management company (socialsharx.com). In addition, she hosts a podcast also entitled Frugalpreneur. Sarah's goal in publishing this book (and the subsequent podcast) is to provide the knowledge she's gained over the years and pass it along to other budding entrepreneurs. When she is not working on her businesses, Sarah likes to read entrepreneurial books, go to concerts, and travel the world.

You can connect with me on:

- https://sarah-stjohn.com
- https://twitter.com/sarahstjohn18
- https://www.facebook.com/thesarahstjohn
- https://www.instagram.com/thesarahstjohn
- https://www.pinterest.com/frugalpreneur
- https://www.spreaker.com/show/frugalpreneur

Also by Sarah St John

If you enjoyed this book, be sure to check out the second book in the Preneur Series out later this year. Available for pre-order now.

Did you know that writing a book is one of the best ways to introduce potential customers to your brand and business? A book gives you instant credibility and authority in your subject matter. People will look at and treat you completely differently once you add "author" to your resume. Think of it as a glorified business card.

But, Houston, we have a problem. You say you have NO idea how to even begin the self publishing process? Fear no more.

It is now easier than ever to self publish a book, but that doesn't mean it doesn't come with its challenges. This book is your guide to simplifying self publishing.

In this book, you will learn:

· How to successfully self publish and launch a book
· How to use a book to help build your business
· Editing tools, software, and resources
· Creating a book cover, typesetting, and formatting
· Print, e-book, and audiobook distribution options
· Bestseller tips and tricks
· Pricing strategies and marketing tactics
· Distributing advanced copies and getting reviews
· Selecting the best categories and keywords in Amazon
· Setting up Amazon Marketing Service (AMS) ads
· Recommended further educational resources

You ready for the challenge? Let's go!

https://books2read.com/b/authorpreneur

Join the Preneur Pack!

For a small annual fee, you can join the Preneur Pack and get access to hundreds of entrepreneurial e-books, software programs, and more! We aren't ready just yet, but if you're interested in being alerted when it launches, please register at:

PreneurPack.com

www.ingramcontent.com/pod-product-compliance
Lightning Source LLC
Chambersburg PA
CBHW071106240526

45469CB00006BD/2354